Hermias

Gentilium Philosophorum Irrisio

Hermias*

Gentilium Philosophorum Irrisio

Christian Apology or Skit on School Homework?

THOMAS P. HALTON

The Catholic University of America

* For Hermias see J. Quasten, *Patrology*, I, Westminster, Md., (1950, rp. 1986), 253, which should be updated from the following recent surveys: *DHGE* XXIV fasc 138, EECh 1, P. Siniscalco, *LThK* 5 (1993) 12, R. Kany, P. T. Camelot, *LThK* 5 (1960) 261, J. A. Fischer, and especially *RAC* XIV (1988) 808–15. The text (with the chapter divisions) used is H. Diels, *Dox Graec.* 649–56, with regular reference to J. C. T. Otto, *Corpus apologetarum christianorum saeculi secundi*, Jena, 1872, vol. 9, XI/LI, 2–31 and, more recently, checked against Hanson. J. H. Waszink, *ANRW* II, 27,4, announced a study of the rapports between *Irrisio* and other patristic authors. On this cf. Hanson, 28–32.

RESOURCE *Publications* • Eugene

HERMIAS, *GENTILIUM PHILOSOPHORUM IRRISIO*
Christian Apology or Skit on School Home-work?

Copyright © 2008 Thomas P. Halton. All rights reserved. Except for brief quotations in critical publications or reviews, no part of this book may be reproduced in any manner without prior written permission from the publisher. Write: Permissions, Wipf and Stock Publishers, 199 W. 8th Ave., Suite 3, Eugene, OR 97401.

Wipf & Stock
A Division of Wipf and Stock Publishers
199 W. 8th Ave., Suite 3
Eugene, OR 97401

www.wipfandstock.com

ISBN 13: 978-1-60608-632-2

Manufactured in the U.S.A.

To Stella

Contents

Acknowledgments ix

Introduction xi

Abbreviations xiii

Translation of *Gentilium Philosophorum Irrisio* 15

Bibliography 45

Acknowledgments

I am grateful to Wipf and Stock for accepting this manuscript for publication, and to Christian Amondson and Diane Farley for plying me with queries about further clarifications; also to copy-editor Genevieve Beenen for prompt and careful collaboration, and to her mentor, Karen J. Torjesen, Dean, Claremont Graduate University, for her recommendation.

Introduction

THIS IS a brand-new translation and commentary of Hermias Diasurmos. I examine Diasurmos as a celebration of Ridicule, which presents to the reader a literary antecedent of Washington Press Club's annual journalists' political Roast.

The present work had its beginnings in a graduate seminar given by this author in the Department of Greek and Latin, The Catholic University of America, shortly after the appearance of Reverend Professor Hanson's critical edition in the Sources Chretiennes series. It benefited from a conversation with Rev. Hanson during a meeting of the quadrennial Patristic Conference in Oxford. As the subtitle—Greek Apology or Skit on School Homework?—suggests, it may be more than a mere satire. In fact, the present study, by a careful sifting of the Greek text and commentary, does furnish new clues to unresolved problems, such as *place of origin* : School of Origen, not of Clement of Alexandria; *date*, somewhat later than 200; and *literary antecedents*, Lucian of Samosata's *Icaromenippus*.

I believe these points are successfully presented and persuasively argued. I also think that the work will enjoy a wide circulation, especially in university libraries.

Witty repartee abounds. Note, for instance, the display of *esprit d'escalier* in his "when I threw myself head-first into the crater, the smoke snatched me out of Aetna."

Introduction

The text is a fast-paced summary of pre-Socratic philosophy and its leaders: Thales, Anaximander, Anaximenes, Anaxagoras, etc.—a glittering lineup of seventeen, all told.

Think of it in modern terms as an end-of-term slideshow presentation, a kind of Moussorgsky's *Pictures at an Exhibition*, in which the examinee flashes photos of the main philosophers accompanied by sound-bites of their teachings on what constitutes the first principle, or starting-point, of the universe (was it water, or fire, or air, etc.) while at the same time allowing a fast-talking, used-car salesman (anything you can say, I can say better) interrupt him with brisk one-liners. In the present work, Lucian, the prolific second-century satiric philosopher, is the exact prototype of the used-car salesman.

I translated it since a reliable, up-to-date version, in an attractive paperback format, is not available, and I have already done the same for similar works, such as Melito's *On the Pasch*, John Chrysostom's *In Praise of St. Paul*, and Jerome's *On Illustrious Men*.

It will be of special interest to professors of early Christianity and their students, to those involved in apologetics, viz., a reasoned presentation of the main tenets of Christianity (the divinity of Christ, his parables, teachings, miracles, death on the cross, resurrection, and ascension), and also to experts on the Greek word παιδεία, *paideia*, on which the German scholar, Werner Jaeger, wrote the classic three-volume: *Paideia: The Ideals of Greek Culture*, translated by G. Highet, and a less satisfactory slim volume titled *Early Christianity and Paideia*.

Abbreviations

ACW	Ancient Christian Writers
Bauckham (1985)	R. Bauckham, "The Fall of the Angels as the Source of Philosophy in Hermias and Clement of Alexandria," *VigChr* 39, 1985, 313–30.
VigChr	*Vigiliae Christianae*.
De Vogel, *GP*	C. J. De Vogel, *Greek Philosophy: A Collection of Texts*, Leiden, Brill, 1959.
Di Pauli, *Die Irrisio*	A. Di Pauli, *Die Irrisio des Hermias*, 1907.
DK	H. Diels and W. Kranz, *Die Fragmente der Vorsokratiker*, Berlin, 1951–1952.
Diels, *Dox. Graec.*	H. Diels, *DoxographiGraeci*, Berlin 1897, 2nd ed., 1929.
FOTC	Fathers of the Church
Freeman, *Ancilla*	K. Freeman, *Ancilla to the Pre Socratic Philosophers*, Harvard University Press, 1952.
Freeman, *Pre-Soc Phil*	K. Freeman, *The Pre Socratic Philosophers*, Oxford, Blackwell, 1966.
Geerard	Geerard, *Clavis Patrum Graecorum*, vol. 1, #111 TLG 0531.
Guthrie, *HGP*	W. Guthrie, *A History of Greek Philosophy*, Cambridge University Press, 1962–1981.

Hanson	*Hermias Satire des Philosophes Paiens* Intro, Texte critique, Notes, Appendices et Index par R. P. C. Hanson et ses collégues Traduction francaise par Denise Joussot, SC 388, Paris, 1993.
Kindstrand (1980)	J. F. Kindstrand, "The Date and Character of Hermias' 'Irrisio,'" *VigChr* 34, 1980, 341–57.
KRS	G. S. Kirk, J. E. Raven, M. Schofield, eds., *The Presocratic Philosophers*, Cambridge University Press, 1983.
LCC	Library of Christian Classics
LCL	Loeb Classical Library
Oct.	*The Octavius of Marcus Minucius Felix*
Origen, *CCels*	Origen, *Contra Celsum*
Osborne *Rethinking*	C. Osborne, *Rethinking Early Greek Philosophy: Hippolytus of Rome and the Presocratics*, Ithaca, NY 1987.
PG	*Patrologia Graeca*
RAC	Reallexikon fur Antike und Christentüm
TLG	Thesaurus Linguae Graecae
Vit. Auct.	Vitarum Auctio
Waterfield	R. Waterfield, tr. *The First Philosophers, The Presocratics and Sophists*, Oxford University Press, 2000.

IN THAT an English translation of Hermias, Diasurmos[1] τῶν ἔξω φιλοσόφων, *Gentilium Philosophorum Irrisio* (Geerard, *CPG* 1113) is not as readily available as R.P.C. Hanson's edition,[2] it may be helpful to provide a working draft here as a basis for some snippets of commentary that hopefully may furnish some new clues to such still unresolved problems as place of origin and date, literary antecedents, and genre. (Is it

---

1. The title word, Diasurmos, is defined in Isidore, "Diasyrmos ea quae magna sunt minuit aut minima extollit," in *Etymol.* II, 21, 43, PL 82, 139. Longinus(?), *On the Sublime* is helpful at a few points in getting a feel for the genre. Comparing Hyperides and Demosthenes, the author says of the former: "There are innumerable signs of wit in him—the most polished raillery, high-bred ease, well-known Attic manner, but naturally suggested by the supple skill in the contests of irony, jests, not tasteless or rude after the subject, clever ridicule (διασυρμοῦ τε ἐπιδέξιος), much comic power, biting satire," chap. 34, ed. W. Rhys Roberts (Cambridge, 1899) 131. And further on: "And, in a sense, ridicule is an amplification of the paltriness of things" (διασυρμοῦ ταπεινοτήτου αὔξησις). See Pseudo-Justin, *Cohort. ad Graec.*, chaps. 3-7 (*FOTC* 6, 377-83) for a similar cataloging. There is a useful synoptic table for the various views in Hanson, 28-32.

2. Hanson mentions (p. 94) two English translations: J. A. Giles, *The Writings of the Early Christians of the Second Century* (London 1857) vii and 193-99 and F. W. M. Hitchcock, "A Skit on Greek Philosophy: By one Hermias, probably of the reign of Julian, A.D. 361-63," *Theology* 32 (1936) 98-106 (which I have read, *pietatis causa,* on Google as a recessional). Other useful translations: L. Alfonsi, *Ermia filosofo,* (Brescia, 1947). [Hanson's bibliography (pp. 91-94) lists nine other items by Alfonsi.] S. Gennaro, *Sullo "Scherno" di Ermia filosofo,* (Catania 1950, 1960). G. A. Rizzo, *Ermia il filosofo, Lo scherno dei filosofi gentili,* (Livorno, 1931) has a good introduction, covering composition, date, models and bibliographical notes, viii-xxxvi.

2 HERMIAS

in any real sense an early Christian Apology?) In particular, the resemblances between Hermias and Lucian of Samosata, especially the latter's *Ikaromenippos*, though they have not gone unnoticed, deserve a fresh look for the light they cast on the literary genre.

TRANSLATION

1

The blessed apostle Paul writing to the Corinthians,
[who sojourned in Laconian Greece][3] declared,
"Beloved ones, the wisdom of this world is absurdity with
 God" (I Cor 3.19, *NAB*).

---

3. Chapter 1 is the only one in Hermias with Christian overtones, leading Kindstrand, "The Date and Character of Hermias' *Irrisio*" (1980) to the perhaps excessively cautious hypothesis that what we have here may be a "secular" satire on the Presocratics, later dressed up with a title and a Pauline quotation (cf. the quotation of 1 Cor 8:1 in *Ad Diognetum* 12,5) by a Christian writer who saw its apologetic potential. Bauckham, "Fall of the Angels" (1985) connects the revolt of the angels reference (Gen. 6:1–4; 1 Enoch 1–36) with something similar in Clement, *Stromata* 3.7,59, which reads: "It actually happened that some angels suffered a failure of self-control, were overpowered by sexual desire and fell to earth," (*FOTC* 85, 292, tr. J. Ferguson).

The awkward phrase *"overpowered by desire for sex, and fell from heaven"* about Laconian Greece is in parentheses in Otto's edition. (See Di Pauli, *Die Irrisio,* 51–52; it seems to suggest an author living outside Greece, probably Asia Minor.) But Lucian, *Icar.* 2, has the phrase ὀρθῶς καὶ οὐκ ἀπὸ σκόπου εἰκάσας, similar to the present οὐκ ἀσκόπως.

Gentilium Philosophorum Irrisio 3

His words were very much to the point; for, in my opinion,

worldly wisdom took its beginning from the revolt of the angels.

That is why the philosophers propose doctrines that are neither

harmonious nor in agreement when they speak one to another.

2

Indeed some of them say that the soul is fire,

others, that it is air,

others intellect,

others motion,

others, an exhalation (ἀναθυμίασις),[4]

others, an energy flowing from the stars,

others, a mobile number,

others, generative water,

others, an element or a composition of elements,

others, a harmony,

others, blood,

others, breath,

others the monad,[5]

---

4. Ps.-Justin, *Cohort. ad Graec.*, chap. 7, is virtually a carbon-copy of the present catalog of various views on the soul.

5. For good measure, Hermias piles on a few more views: *others an*

4 HERMIAS

and the ancients, contrary elements.

How many explanations have been given on this subject,
how many dialectical ratiocinations,
how many judgments of sophists, who contend about,
rather than discover, the truth!

---

element or a combination of elements, others a harmony, others blood, others breath, others the monad, and the ancients contrary elements. Among Justin's works, Eusebius, *H.E.* IV, 18, 5 lists a disputation, *On the Soul* (*LCL*, 371) in which he propounds various questions regarding the problem involved and cites the opinions of the Greek philosophers (noted in Di Pauli.52). This was probably the information base for the present chapter, and perhaps for other parts of the present work. Another possible source might be the work, *To Tatian, On the Soul*, sometimes ascribed to Gregory Thaumaturgus.

The best commentary on chap. 2 is found in Nemesius, *De Natura Hominis* (*PG* 40, 536–37), which conveniently supplies some of the appropriate Presocratic names for each theory; cf. Teubner ed., M. Morani (Leipzig, 1987) 16–17; tr. W. Telfer, *LCC* 4 (Philadelphia, 1954) 257–59. See M. C. Nussbaum, "Psyche in Heraclitus," *Phronesis* 17 (1972) 1–16, 153–70 for useful lexical background, also M. Morani, "*Nemesiana parva*," *Orpheus* 8 (1987) 144–48, esp. 147–48. For other instances of ἀναθυμίασις see Diels, *Dox. Graec.* 716 s.v. Heraclitus, on the other hand, supposes that the soul of the universe is an exhalation of vapor, ἀναθυμίασις. See Nemesius, *De Nat. Hom.* 1 (*PG* 40. 504) notes, 87. Whatever the merits of that distinction—[cf. H. Blumenthal, "Nous and Soul in Plotinus," in *Plotino e il Neoplatonismo* (1974) 203–19 and "Soul, World-Soul and Individual Soul in Plotinus"—in *Le Néoplatonisme* (Paris, 1971)]—it is obvious that Hermias had no awareness of Plotinus or Neoplatonism, an indication, it seems safe to say, that he predates them.

3

Be that as it may! They are in contention with regard to the soul.

But with regard to the questions that concern it,

[surely?] they spoke in agreement.

Some call the pleasure of the soul [one thing, others another]:

one calls it a good,

a second one, an evil,

a third, an intermediary between good and evil.

Some say that the nature of the soul is immortal,

others, that it is mortal,

others, that it survives [after death] for a little while,

others transform it into beasts,

others dissolve it into atoms,

others re-incarnate it three times,

others limit it to a cycle of three thousand years[6]

---

6. The necessary backdrop here is provided by Plato, *Phaedo* 114 d. A *reductio ad absurdum* of metempsychosis, delivered in the senate resolution in Lucian's *Menippus* (chap. 20), is also relevant: "Be it resolved that their souls be sent back into life and enter into donkeys until they shall have passed two hundred and fifty thousand years in the said condition, transmigrating from donkey to donkey."

In Justin's *Trypho*: "As a punishment," I answered, "they will be imprisoned in the bodies of certain wild beasts."

Lucian, *The Dream* or *The Cock*, 19–20 (*LCL* 2, 212) is a clever spoof on multiple transmigration:

Micyllus: They say that while you were Pythagoras, and young and

6 HERMIAS

and indeed people who do not live even for a hundred years make pronouncements about a future of three thousand years.

4

How, then, should we characterize these views? In my view, portentous humbug, nonsense, frenzied chaos, or all of these.[7]

---

handsome, you often played Aspasia to the tyrant. But what man or woman did you become after Aspasia?

Cock: The Cynic Crates.

Micyllus: Twin brethren! What ups and downs! First a courtesan, then a philosopher.

Cock: Then a king, then a poor man, next a satrap; then a horse, a jackdaw, a frog, and a thousand things besides.

7. The opening sentence sounds like *ad Diognetum,* 8,4: Now these things are the miracle-mongering and deceit of the magicians (τερατεία καὶ πλάνη τῶν γοήτων). The remark "I have dolphins for brothers" receives a neat gloss in Lucian in this exchange between Poseidon and a dolphin:

Poseidon: It's greatly to the credit of you dolphins that you've always been kind to men. Long ago you caught up Ino's son after his fall from the cliffs. And now one of you has picked up this harper from Methymna (i.e., Arion; cf. Herodotus I. 23–24).

Dolphin: Don't be surprised, Poseidon, that we are kind to men. We were men ourselves before we became fish. It wasn't very nice of Dionysius to change our shape after he'd beaten us in that sea-battle, "Dialogues of the Sea-Gods," 5 (8).

Lucian also refers to Arion's rescue by dolphins (*Naut.* 19). See further W. Burkert, "The Return of the Dolphin," in *Homo Necans: the anthropology of ancient Greek sacrificial ritual and myth* (Berkeley, CA., 1983) 196–204.

The chimera is also a frequent guest in Lucian. Dionysius of Sicily is on the verge of being chained to him, and the chimera and Cerberus

Gentilium Philosophorum Irrisio 7

If they have discovered some truth let them be of one mind,

or give assent to the same opinions,

and then I myself would gladly be persuaded by them.

But if they tear and drag apart the soul in opposite directions (ἐστασίαζον),

one to one substance, another to another,

and alter one substance after another [i.e. on the composition of the soul],

then I confess that I am exceedingly grieved

by the ebb and flow of [these] matters.

At one time I am immortal and rejoice;

next thing I become mortal and weep.

Presently I am dissolved into atoms.

I become water, I become air, I become fire.

The philosopher makes me a beast, makes me a fish,

next thing I have dolphins for brothers.

Whenever I see myself,

I am afraid of my body and I do not know what to call it:

dragon, man, or dog, or wolf, or bull, or bird, or serpent, or chimera,[8]

---

are tearing and ravening (ἐσπάραττεν, ἐδάρδαπτεν) at the sound of scourges, *Menipp*, 14. See also *pseudol* (On Lucian, see Liddell Scott Jones, p. xxviii); *Hermotimus* 72; *Menippus* 14; *DMort.* 450.

8. Even more strikingly, it sounds like the exchange between Menippus and his friend in Lucian,

Icar: Extraordinary that learned men quarreled with each other about their doctrines (ἐστασίαζον) and did not hold the same views

for, according to the philosophers, I change into all of the beasts:

land- and water- and winged-beasts,

manifold, wild and tame, mute and articulate, irrational and rational.

I swim, I fly, I creep, I run, I sit.

And, what is more, Empedocles makes me a bush.[9]

5

Very good! Since the philosophers cannot arrive at unanimity

about the human soul, still less can they give a true opinion

about the gods and the world.

And, truly, they have this much solidity, not to call it stolidity,

---

about the same things.

Menippus: Indeed, my friend, it will make you laugh to hear about their bragging and wonder-working (ἀλαζονείαν, τερατουργίαν) in their talk!

For Empedocles of Acragas in Sicily, see fr. B117 *DK* [= Fr. 34 Zuntz]; quoted also in Hippolytus, *Ref.* 1.3: (ed. Marcovich, 62); Guthrie, *HGP* vol. 2. 250; C. Osborne, *Rethinking,* 87–131.

9. Hippolytus, *Ref.* 1, iii, 2, says: Above all, [Empedocles] assents to the idea of metempsychosis, saying: "For already I have once been a boy and a girl, and a bush and a bird and a silent fish in the sea." Origen, *CCels.,* Empedocles teaches "the soul must wander about, away from the blessed, for thirty thousand years, becoming in its time every possible shape of mortal being," *Celsus on the True Doctrine,* tr. R. J. Hoffmann (Oxford 1987) 122. For an extensive array of texts on metempsychosis, see *KRS*, chap. X.

that, being unable to discover the nature of their own soul,
they seek to understand that of their gods,
and people who do not know the nature of their own body
labor over the nature of the world.

6

At any rate, they stand wholly at odds with one another
on what is the first principle of nature:
that mind is the cause and master of the universe,
that it provides order for what is disordered.
Whenever Anaxagoras[10] accepts me as a pupil, I learn this:
"The first principle of all things is Mind,
providing motion for what is motionless,
separation for what is intermingled,
and beauty for what is ugly."[11]
When Anaxagoras makes these statements,
I cherish him and am persuaded by his teaching.

---

10. For Anaxagoras (c.500–428 B.C.) see *DK* 59 [46] esp. 59A1, 59B12; Freeman, *Ancilla* 82–86; *Pre-Soc Phil,* 261–74; *KRS* 352–84; Guthrie, *HGP* vol. 2, 266–338, esp. 272f; Hippolytus, *Ref.* 1.8. Origen, *CCels.* 7, 36 mentions A.'s "wise maxims." Kindstrand (1980) 345–47 finds similarities between this προσωποποιΐα of Anaxagoras and Maximus of Tyre.

11. Waterfield, 116–32.

But Melissus[12] and Parmenides[13] take their stand against him.

And Parmenides heralds abroad with poetical verse:

"Being is one, eternal, infinite, immovable, and perfectly identical in itself."[14]

Here I am once again.

In this teaching I do not know how to change.

Parmenides has chased Anaxagoras out of my mind.

7

Then, when I think that I have an unshakeable doctrine,

Anaximene,[15] interjecting, cries out in turn:

---

12. For Melissus cf. Waterfield, 82–86; De Vogel, *GP* 1. 49–50; *KRS* 390–401; L. Sweeney, *Infinity in the Pre-Socratics*, 124–35. Parmenides (c.520–c.450 B.C.) and Melissus are linked as here in Sextus Empiricus, *Pyrrh.* III.65, as opposed to the prevalent view that motion (κίνησις) exists; cf. Aristotle, *Phys.* 1.2.185/b–186b.

13. For Parmenides, cf. Waterfield, 49–68.

14. The Parmenides quotation is from *DK*, fragment 8.3; on which see Scott Austin, *Parmenides Being, Bound and Logic* (New Haven and London, Yale University Press, 1986) 162–63, (text and trans.), A. H. Coxon, *The Fragments of Parmenides* (Assen 1986) 60–61, 193–226, D. Gallop, *Parmenides of Elea, Fragments* (Toronto 1984) 64–65, 98–100; A. P. D. Mourelatos, *The Route of Parmenides* (New Haven and London 1970) 94–111, 281; L. Taran, *Parmenides* (Princeton, NJ. 1965) 82, 85f. See also Freeman, *Ancilla* 48, *KRS* 239–62. This should be compared with what Hippolytus has to say of Xenophanes, in *Ref.* 1.14. See also D. Furley, "Anaxagoras in Response to Parmenides" in: J. P. Anton and A. Preus, eds. *Essays in Ancient Greek Philosophy* 2 vols. (Albany, N.Y. 1983) 70–92.

15. For Anaximenes, (c.) see *DK* 13, *Dox Graec.* 278; Nemesius,

"But I tell you, the universe is air and this,

when it becomes thick and condensed,

becomes water and earth;

when it is rarefied and diffuse,

it becomes ether and fire;

and, returning to its own nature, it becomes air."[16]

It undergoes alteration, he says,

when it is evaporated and condensed.

And once again I am corrected by him and I love
 Anaximenes.

8

But Empedocles,[17] snorting indignantly and explosively
 from Mount Aetna, says,

"First principles of all things are love and strife;

the first, uniting all things together, and the second separating them,

and the conflict of these makes all things."

I define these things made by love and strife as like and
 unlike,

DNH, chap. 5; Freeman, *Ancilla* 19; De Vogel, *GP* vol. 1. 8–9; Guthrie, *HGP*. vol. 1, 115–40; *KRS*, 143–45.

16. On Anaximenes, Waterfield, 3–21; *DK*, 93.

17. For Empedocles (c. 495–c.435 B.C.) cf. Waterfield, 133–63; De Vogel *GP* 1. 51–64, esp. 54–59; *KRS* 280–87. For his suicide, see *DK* 31, *ox. Graec.* 478; Guthrie, *HGP* vol. 2, 152; Lactantius, *Div. Inst.* 3, 18.

as infinite and finite, as eternal, and coming to be.[18]

Well done, Empedocles! I follow you right up to the craters of the fire.

9

But Protagoras,[19] having taken his stand on the other side,

draws me aside, saying,

"Man is the limit and measure of the things that exist.

And whatever pertains to the senses,

these are the things that exist;

---

18. Empedocles' views are described in almost identical terms in ps.-Justin, *Cohort. ad Graec.* 4 (*FOTC* 6, 378–79). See also Hippolytus, *Ref.* 1.3.1 (ed. Markovich, 62); also J. B. Herbshell, (1973) 97–114, 187–203, esp. 197–98, 103–4. Hermias's "following him to the edge of the crater" is more than matched in Lucian, *DMort.* 416:

Menippus: Who is this covered with cinders, like a loaf baked in the ashes?

Aeacus: Empedocles; he came half-boiled from Aetna.

Menippus: O brazen foot [cf. Strabo VI. 274, DiogL VIII 69] what came over you that you jumped into the crater?

Empedocles: A fit of mad depression, Menippus.

Menippus: No, but a fit of vanity and pride and a dose of driveling folly.

He also shows up in *Icar*, 13: "I am the natural philosopher Empedocles. You see, when I threw myself head-first into the crater the smoke snatched me out of Aetna, and brought me up here . . . and now I dwell in the moon, although I walk the air a great deal, and I live on dew (*LCL* ed., vol. II, 291, cf. *loc. cit.*, 289). See further J. Hall, *Lucian's Satire* (New York 1981) 165.

19. For Protagoras (490–c.420 B.C.), see *Dox. Graec.*, 396; DK 80 A16, 253–71, esp. 257–59; *KRS* 258, 13; Waterfield, 205–21; Freeman, *Pre-Soc Phil.* 343–48; M. Untersteiner, *The Sophists* (Oxford 1954) 1–91, esp. 77–91.

whatever does not pertain to them,

these do not exist among the species of being."[20]

I am flattered by this account and delighted by Protagoras,

since the universe, or the greater part of it,

is dealt out and handled by man.

10

From another side, Thales[21] beckons me with an emphatic nod;

he defines water as the true first principle of the universe.

"And all things are composed from moisture and dissolve into moisture;

even the earth is carried upon water."[22]

Well now; why should I not be persuaded by Thales,

---

20. The Protagoras quotation is a paraphrase; it may have been suggested by Plato, *Theaetetus* 152a., 160d. or *Crat*. 385e–386a. See L. Alfonsi, "L'<uomo> di Protagora in Ermia"; *RSF* 1 (1946) 320–21 and *idem*, "Protagora <adulatore>"; *ASNP* ser. 2, 16 (1947) 193–94. Alfonsi sees an allusion to Eupolis, *The Flatterers*. And by interpreting Protagoras as rejecting Love, Discord and Water as first principles of nature and replacing them by Man himself, Alfonsi thinks Hermias somehow anticipates the philosopher Berkeley. See also A. Levi, "Studies on Protagoras. The man-measure principle: its meaning and applications," *Philosophy* 15 (1940) 147–67.

21. The "oldest of the Ionians": in ps.-Justin, *Cohort. ad Graec*. 3, Thales is called "that pioneer student of natural philosophy." He is treated out of sequence here by Hermias, who is obviously following no particular chronological order and not trying to be exhaustive. See *KRS*, 76–99.

22. Thales: *DK* pp. 83–84; Waterfield, 3–21.

the oldest of the Ionians?

But his fellow-countryman, Anaximander,[23] says:

"Eternal motion is an older first principle than water

and it is in virtue of this that coming to be and passing away exist."[24]

And now indeed, let Anaximander be the one whom I believe.

11

But here comes Archelaus.[25]

What a dashing figure he cuts as he proclaims

that hot and cold are the first principles of the universe.

But, once again, the loud-voiced Plato[26] disagrees;

23. Elsewhere (e.g. ps.-Justin, *Cohort. ad Graec.*, 3) Anaximander is assigned the more familiar label, Apeiron; cf. P. Seligman, *The Apeiron of Anaximander* (London 1962); Th. G. Sinnige, *Matter and Infinity in the Presocratic Schools and Plato* (Assen 1968); L. Sweeney, *Infinity in the Presocratics* (The Hague, 1972) 1–54; C. H. Kahn, *Anaximander and the Origins of Greek Cosmology* (New York, 1964); Waterfield, 3–21; R. M. Dancy, "Thales, Anaximander and infinity," *Apeiron* 22, 3 (1989) 149–90.

24. Anaximander gets a much fuller treatment in Hippolytus, *Ref.* 1,6 (ed. Marcovich, 64–65). See also *DK*, pp. 83–84; *KRS* 100–142.

25. On Archelaus, successor of Anaxagoras, see Aetius, I,3,6; I, 7,14; 11, 4, 5, 111.3, 5, IV,3,5; *KRS,* chap. XIII, 385–89; Diog L II, 17 (= *DK* 60 A 1). In ps.-Justin, *Cohort. ad Graec.* 3 we read: "The Athenian, Archelaus, . . . says that the infinite air, with its density and rarity, is the first principle of all things" (*FOTC* 6, 378). For a fuller account, see Hippolytus *Ref.* 1.9, τὸ μὲν θερμὸν κινεῖσθαι, τὸ δὲ ψυχρὸν ἠρεμεῖν [= *DK*, cf. Plato, *Soph.* 242cd].

26. Plato is also μεγαλόφωνος in ps.-Justin, *Cohort. ad Graec.* 31,

he says that the first principles are God, matter, and forms.[27]

And now here I am, one more time, convinced.

For, how shall I not believe the philosopher

who manufactured the chariot of Zeus?[28]

But his pupil, Aristotle,[29] stands behind him,

jealous of the teacher of chariot-making.

He defines different first principles: "the active, and the passive."

And the active makes the ether impassible;

the passive has four qualities: dryness, moistness, heat and cold.

---

where he is introduced speaking of Zeus's winged chariot; doubtless this is Hermias' source here (cf. Di Pauli, *Die Irrisio,* 17–20).

27. In ps.-Justin, *Cohort. ad Graec.* 6, Plato is also credited with believing in these same three principles: "Plato states that, next to God and matter, form is the third of the original principles of things," (*FOTC* 6, 382). See also Aetius, *Plac.* 1,7,4, (cf. Di Pauli, *Die Irrisio,* 15–20; art. "Hermias," *RAC* XIV, 812).

28. The chariot of Zeus, described in Plato, *Phaedrus* 246a–247b, became an extremely popular text. For extensive references cf. J. Geffcken, *Zwei griechische Apologeten* (Leipzig 1907) 213; M. Marcovich, ed. *Athenagoras, Legatio pro Christianis* (PTS 31, Berlin, New York 1990) 77 [on *Leg.* 23,4]. See further A. Méasson, *Du char ailé de Zeus à l'Arche d'Alliance; images et mythes platoniciens chez Philon d'Alexandrie* [diss. Lyon 1982] (Paris 1986); bibliog. 415–24 Lucian's *A Professor of Public Speaking* ends with Plato's famous phrase: "[D]riving in a winged chariot can be applied by you to yourself with a better grace than by Plato himself to Zeus."

29. Plato and Aristotle are differentiated from the Presocratics in ps.-Justin, *Cohort. ad Graec.* 5 as potentially better guides, only to be quickly devaluated for their contradictory views.

By the alteration of these into each other, all things come into being and perish.[30]

12

By now, we are weary, as we undergo the ups and downs, the vacillations of these views;

unless I take my stand with the opinion of Aristotle, and not allow one single argument trouble me any longer.

So what should I do now? For elders more ancient than these tug at the strings of my soul.

Pherecydes[31] says: "The first principles are Zeus, and Chthonia, and Chronos.

Zeus who is the air, Chthonia, earth, and Chronos, time.

Air is the active principle, earth is the one acted upon,

and time, that in which things come to be."[32]

Well now, emulation is alive and well among the elders.

For Leucippus[33] considering all of these things to be humbug, says:

---

30. For Aristotle, cf. De Vogel, *GP* vol. 2, 67–101.

31. For an extended introduction to Pherecydes, see M. L. West, *Early Greek Philosophy and the Orient* (Oxford 1971) 1–75, esp. 9–20 and *KRS*, 50–71, esp. 56.

32. Origen, *CCels.*, 6,42, quotes Pherecydes, frags. 4 and 5; cf. *Celsus on the True Doctrine*, tr. R. J. Hoffmann, 99–100.

33. Leucippus gets a similar treatment in Hippolytus, *Ref.* 1.12 (ed. Markovich, 72). See also *KRS,* 402–9; Nemesius, *De Nat Hom*, 1,64, ed. Morani, 15, l.6.

Gentilium Philosophorum Irrisio 17

"The first principles are the infinite, the perpetual motion, and the most minute;

whatever consists of most delicate parts moves up to become fire and air;

whatever consists of thick and coarse parts descends below as water and earth."[34]

13

How long shall I be taught such a number of things and never learn the truth?

Unless perhaps Democritus[35] release me a bit from my straying, when he proclaims:

"The first principles are being and non-being;

and being is full, non-being is empty.

The full in the empty, by turns and by measures,

makes all of the things that are."[36]

Perhaps I might have been persuaded by the noble Democritus

and I would have liked to share a laugh with him,

---

34. On Leucippus, cf. Waterfield, 164–93.

35. The juxtaposition of the "laughing" and "weeping" philosophers may well have been lifted from Lucian, *De sacrificiis* 15 (cf. Di Pauli, *Die Irrisio*, 41). Also in Lucian, *Vit. Auct.* 13, "the one from Abdera who laughs and the one from Ephesus who weeps" constitute a bargain in a two-for-one sale.

36. Democritus, cf. De Vogel, *GP*, 1, 70, quoting Aristotle, *Metaph.* A4, 985b; Waterfield, 164–93.

except that Heraclitus[37] stands near me and weeps;

he persuades me otherwise and says,

"Fire is the first principle of the Universe;

it has two states: evaporation and condensation.

The first is active and the other is acted upon;

the first, brings together, the other, disperses."[38]

This is enough for me and I'm already intoxicated by such grand first principles.

14

But then Epicurus[39] exhorts me in no way to spurn and insult

his beautiful doctrine of atoms and void:

"By the multiform and variegated intertwining of these,

all things come to be and pass away."[40]

---

37. For Heraclitus (c.540–c.480 B.C), T. M. Robinson, ed. *Heraclitus Fragments* (Toronto 1987) for fragments in Hippolytus cf. Osborne, *Rethinking*, 132–82 and also *KRS* 181–212.

38. Heraclitus, Waterfield, 32–48.

39. For Epicurus, cf. De Vogel, *GP* 3, 4–43.

40. On the infinite worlds of Epicurus see De Vogel, *GP* 3.20; Origen, *CCels.* 2,13, 4,14; 4.75; 4,886. For atoms and the void cf. Hippolytus, *Ref.* 1,22,1 (ed. Marcovich 84). Minucius Felix, *Oct.* 5,7 speaks of "the chance collision of atoms (fortuitous concourses or collisions; on which see G. W. Clarke, *ACW* 39, 185, n.45.

In W. G. Englert, *Epicurus on the Swerve and Voluntary Action* (Atlanta 1987) 30, we read: "Aristotle *De coelo* III, 4 303a5 =*KRS* 579 informs us that two things can happen after atoms collide: (1) atoms can collide and then jump apart (περιπαλάσσονται), each heading off in

I do not contradict you, my good fellow, Epicurus.

But the head of Cleanthes[41] emerges from his well

and he laughs at your teaching;

on his own he dredges up from the well:

"The true first principles are god and matter."[42]

And he says that the earth changes into water while water changes into air;

air is borne upward; fire goes up to the peripheral;

the soul pervades the whole universe;

a portion of which we share in and are thereby animated.

15

Numerous though these philosophers are, I am over-run

---

new directions which they maintain until they again collide with other atoms, or (2) they can 'cohere' or 'intertwine' (συμπλοκή), and travel on together to be struck by other atoms, which either cohere to them, rebound off, or break them apart."

41. Cleanthes of Assos (331–232 B.C.) was a pupil and successor of Zeno of Citium, Cyprus, founder of Stoicism. Minucius Felix, *Oct.* 19,9 reads: "Cleanthes argued sometimes that God is mind and soul, sometimes that He is ether, and frequently that he is reason" (tr. G. W. Clarke, *ACW* 39, 84, and 270, n. 253).

42. We learn from Diogenes Laertius (VII. 5, 168), that Cleanthes was driven by extreme poverty to work for a living. By night he used to draw water in gardens (ἐν τοῖς κήποις ἤντλει); by day he exercised himself in arguments: hence his nickname, Φρεάντλης, Phreantles, or Well-lifter. See further "Kleanthes" Pauly-Wissowa Kroll, Realencyclopadie, XI/I (1921) 561f, A. C. Pearson, ed., *The Fragments of Zeno and Cleanthes* (London 1891) 250–51.

by another crowd—from Libya:[43] Carneades, and
  Clitomachus,[44]

and all their followers, stampeding over all the doctrines of
the others,

and declaring with legal precision:

43. On Libya one recalls Aristotle, *Hist. Anim.*, VII (VIII): LCL 202: "In general, the wild animals are wilder in Asia, but all those in Europe are braver, while those in Libya are the most varied in form; in fact, there is a proverb that Libya ever bears something new." On Libya synonymous with Africa cf. Origen, *CCels.*; Theodoret, *ep.* XXII: ἡ πάλαι Λιβύη, νῦν δὲ Ἀφρική καλουμένη (SC 40,93 and n.1).

44. On Carneades (c.219–c.129 B.C.) and Clitomachos (c.187–c.110 B.C.) see R. J. Hankinson, *The Sceptics*, (London/New York, 1995) 94–116. Sextus Empiricus, *Outlines of Pyrrhonism* I. 220 helps to place the Libyans in context: "According to most people there have been three Academies—first, Plato and his school, second or Middle, that of Archesilaos . . . the third or New Academy, that of the School of Carneades and Clitomachus." At the outset of his *Outlines* he has something even more germane to the present treatise (I. 1-4.): "The natural result of any investigation is that the investigators either discover the object of search, or deny that it is discoverable and profess its ungraspability (ἀκαταληψία), or persist in their search. [In philosophy] those who believe that they have discovered it are the 'Dogmatists,' specially so-called—Aristotle, for example, and Epicurus, and the Stoics and certain others. Clitomachus and Carneades and other Academics treat it as ungraspable (ἀκατάληπτον): the Sceptics keep on searching." Likewise, Cicero helps to pinpoint the contributions of Carneades and Clitomachus to philosophy: "I agree with Clitomachus when he writes that Carneades really did accomplish an almost Herculean labor in ridding our minds of that fierce wild beast, the act of assent, that is of mere opinion and hasty thinking," (*Acad.* II.108). In *Rhet.* II. 20, Sextus Empiricus reports that "the men of the Academy, including Clitomachos and Charmides (both disciples of Carneades), are wont to argue like this—that the cities do not expel the arts, knowing them to be extremely useful for life. The New Academy, then, combined Critical Scepticism and Probabilism."

"The universe is incomprehensible; alongside of the truth
there is a false phantasm."[45]

Well now, why do I suffer so long in hard labor?

How can I dredge such enormous quantities of bilgy opinion
out of my mind?

For if nothing is comprehensible, then the truth is vanished
from among men;

and our celebrated philosophy shadowboxes with,

rather than gains possession of, the true knowledge of being.

16

Others, then, from the ancient school, Pythagoras[46]

and his fellow tribesmen, solemn and silent,

transmit other dogmas to me as mysteries,

and this is the great and ineffable "Quoth he"[47]:

45. On the "phantasy" cf. Sextus Empiricus, *Against the Logicians,* "We cannot admit every presentation (φαντασία) as a criterion of truth, but—if any—only that which is true. So then, once more, since there is no true presentation (φαντασία) of such a kind that it cannot be false, but a false presentation is found to exist exactly resembling every apparently true presentation, the criterion will consist of a presentation which contains the true and the false alike. But the presentation which contains them both is not apprehensive and, not being apprehensive (μὴ οὖσα καταληπτική) it will not be a criterion," I: 163–65. See further De Vogel, *GP* vol. 3. 200–218; Diogenes Laertius, IV. 9 and 10; A. A. Long, *Hellenistic Philosophy* (London 1974) 94–106 (cited by Hanson, p.113). Lucian, *Hermot* 33 also talks of shadow-boxing (σκιαμαχία).

46. Waterfield, 87–115; D. J. O'Meara, *Pythagoras revived: Mathematics and philosophy in late antiquity* (New York, 1990).

47. Cf. Gregory Nazianzus, *Oratio* 27,10: "Attack the silence of

"The Monad is the first principle of all things.

From its forms and from numbers the elements are born."[48]

And he declares that the number, form and measure of each of these

is somehow as follows:[49]

Pythagoras, or the Orphic beans, or the extraordinary pretentiousness of 'Thus spake the Master,'" tr. L. Wickham / F. Williams, in F. W. Norris, *Faith Gives Fullness to Reasoning: The Five Theological Orations of Gregory Nazianzen* (Leiden 1991) 223.

48. Cf. ps.-Justin, *Cohort. ad Graec.*, 4: "Pythagoras . . . considers numbers, with their proportion and harmony, and their resultant elements, as the basis of things. In his system he also includes the unity (μονάς) and infinite duality of numbers," (*FOTC* 6, 376).

49. The translation of this difficult chapter has been greatly facilitated by K. S. Guthrie, *The Pythagorean Sourcebook and Library* (Phanes Press 1987) which has helpful drawings of the various figures, tetrahedron, icosahedron, etc. Also helpful is M. C. Nahm, *Selections from Early Greek Philosophy* (New York 1964) 59, which prints the following excerpt from Aetius, *placita* II. 6. [Dox. 334] on which Hermias is obviously based: [Pythagoras]: "The universe is made from five solid figures, which are called also mathematical; of these he says that earth has arisen from the cube, fire from the pyramid, air from the octahedron, and water from the icosahedron, and the sphere of the all from the dodecahedron." See also J. C. Thom, "The Journey Up and Down: Pythagoras in Two Greek Apologists," *ChH* 58 (1989) 299–308 [Theophilus, *Ad Autol.* 3,7; *Irrisio*, 16–17.]; also *KRS* 214–38.

L. Alfonso ingeniously sees here a parody of Plato, *Theaetetus*, 173e which reads: "If the philosopher holds aloof it is because it is really only his body that sojourns in his city, while his thought, disdaining all such things as worthless, takes wings, as Pindar says, beyond the sky, beneath the earth, searching the heavens and measuring the plains, everywhere, seeking the true nature of everything as a whole, never sinking to what lies close at hand." Hanson finds echoes of Plato, *Apol.* 31b, in the opening ἔκφρασις of the philosopher abandoning family and the cares of the world to pursue his study single-mindedly (SC 388,56). His section—*la géometrie pythagoricienne* (p. 57 and Appendix IV, 133–

Fire is composed of twenty-four right-angled triangles, surrounded by four equilaterals, and each equilateral consists of six right-angled triangles whence they compare it to the pyramid.

Air is composed of forty-eight triangles surrounded by eight equilaterals.

And it is compared to the octahedron, which is surrounded by eight equilateral triangles,

---

38)—is particularly helpful.

Enthusiasm also characterizes Menippus at the beginning of Lucian, *Icarus*: "and trivial and insecure (wealth, I mean, and office and sovereign power) contemning these things and assuming that the effort to get them was an obstacle to getting things done truly worth effort I undertook to lift my eyes and contemplate the universe." Lucian also has thoughts of ascending to heaven in *Icar.* to break his philosophical impasse: "I did not know where to turn in order to find a point of doctrine that was unassailable and not in any way subject to refutation by someone else. At my wit's end I despaired of hearing any truth about these matters on earth and thought that the only way out of my whole dilemma would be to get wings somehow and go up to Heaven."

Hermias's going into orbit is obviously inspired by his previous mention (chap. 10) of the chariot of Zeus. He now simply becomes his own winged charioteer. The time-span of "a single day" may have been suggested by the opening of Lucian, *Icar.*: "It was three thousand furlongs, then, from the earth to the moon, my first stage; and from there up to the sun perhaps five hundred leagues; and from the sun to Heaven itself and the citadel of Zeus would be also a day's ascent for an eagle traveling light." The measurements in finger lengths may also be explained by the finger lengths in Lucian, *Icarus,* rather than by those in Isaiah 40:12 (LXX) (*pace* Hanson, SC 388, 21–22): "As a matter of fact, since the whole of Greece as it looked to me then from on high was no bigger than four fingers, on that scale surely Attica was infinitesimal."

Alfonsi, "In Hermiam Adnotatiuncula," *Mondo Classico* n.s.2 (1948) 34–35 sees an echo of Aristophanes, *Clouds* 201 f.

each of which is separated into six right-angled triangles so as to become forty-eight in all.

And water is composed of one hundred and twenty triangles, surrounded by twenty equilaterals,

and it is compared to the icosahedron, which is composed of one hundred and twenty equilateral triangles.

And aether is composed of twelve equilateral pentagons, and is like a dodecahedron.

And earth is composed of forty-eight triangles, and is surrounded by six equilateral tetragons,

and it is like a cube. For the cube is surrounded by six tetragons,

each of which is divided into eight triangles so that in all they add up to forty-eight.

17

Pythagoras, then, measures the universe. And in my newfound enthusiasm I turn my back on home,

fatherland, wife and children; I am no longer concerned about them.

Then I make my ascent into the very aether and, taking the cubit measure from Pythagoras,[50]

---

50. On the cubit measure Theodoret, *Curatio* 1. 97–98 is playfully sarcastic: "And again, there is a great war of words between them concerning the sun. Anaximander and Anaximenes asserted that it was twenty-seven times larger than the earth. For Anaxagoras, it was larger than the Peloponnese, and Heraclitus of Ephesus thought it was a foot in diameter. Who would not rightly laugh at such divergences of view?

Gentilium Philosophorum Irrisio 25

I start measuring the fire. For Zeus falls short when it comes to measuring, and if I,

great character that I am, great in body, great in soul, were not to ascend into heaven to measure the aether,

the rule of Zeus would come to an end.

Having finished my measuring and briefing of Zeus about how many angles fire has,

I again descend from heaven, gulp down a few olives, figs and vegetables as fast as I can,

and then I am off at full speed to the water.

I measure the watery substance in cubits, inches and half-inches.

I plumb its depths in order to teach Poseidon as well the extent of his nautical domain.

I survey the whole earth in a single day, collecting its statistics, measurements and shapes.

For I am convinced that I, being such a marvelous character, will not overlook

even a single finger-span of the entire universe.

I also know the number of the stars, fish and animals,

and once I have placed the universe on a scale I can easily learn its weight.[51]

And the differences of infinity about which mere words cannot give an adequate idea. For who, in fact, could encompass the whole world with a measure and then, having multiplied it by twenty-seven, contract the measure of the counter and compare this to the measurement of a man's foot?" (SC 57, 129).

51. Gregory Nazianzus, *Oratio* has a similar conceit: "Movingly

18

My soul has up to now busied itself with these concerns to get the measure of the universe.

But Epicurus, leaning forward,[52] says to me:

"My friend, you have merely measured a single world, but there are many, unlimited worlds."[53]

So, once more I am compelled to measure other heavens, other upper airs, and these are numerous.

So, without further ado, having gathered provisions sufficient for a few days,

I will embark on a tour of the worlds of Epicurus.

I will easily soar over the boundaries, Thetis and Oceanus.[54]

---

holy David has meditated on our weakness." And again in the words, "Declare unto me the fewness of my days"; and he defines the days of man as a finger-breadth measure.

52. Epicurus' gesture of "leaning forward" (προκύψας) is replicated (ἐπέκυψε,) in Lucian, *Jup.* 33 when the gods and Zeus give a general audience to the agnostics, Damis and Tomocles. Even more striking is Lucian, *Menippus* 21, where Menippus is consulting Teiresias on the nature of the good life. "After initial hesitation, because Rhadamanthus does not authorize such exchange, Teiresias took me aside, and after he had led me a good way from the others, he bent his head slightly towards my ear and said, 'The life of the common sort is best and you will act more wisely if you stop speculating about heavenly bodies and discussing final causes and first causes, spit your scorn at those clever syllogisms, and, counting all that sort of thing nonsense, make it always your sole object to put the present to good use and to hasten on your way, laughing a great deal and taking nothing seriously.'"

53. For Epicurus' unlimited worlds, cf. *Diog.* X. 45; De Vogel, *GP* vol. 3. 20.

54. An echo of Homer, *Il.* 14. 201, 302, a line quoted also in Plato, *Theaet.* 152e, 180d.

Entering a new world, just like entering a new city, I will measure the whole in a few days.

And from there I fly on to a third world, then a fourth, a fifth, a tenth, a twentieth, a thousandth, and so on.

Already the darkness of ignorance was coming upon me, and black deceit,

and unlimited error, and ineffectual fantasy, and incomprehensible folly.

Why, I am about to count the atoms themselves, from which so many worlds have come into existence,

so as to leave nothing unexamined of what is most necessary and beneficial

that contributes to the happiness of domestic and civic life.

19

Accordingly I have explored those theories,

wishing to show how opposed they are to one another in their views,

how their research into reality is limitless and endless,

and their object imprecise, useless,

confirmed by no manifest achievement or meaningful argument.[55]

---

55. A similarly agnostic conclusion is announced in ps.-Justin, *Cohort. ad Graec.* 4: "You can readily perceive the confusion that exists among those who you say are your wise men—whom you call your teachers of religion . . . all of them used specious arguments to prove their unsound teachings." Lucian, *Hermot.* ends with a similar repudiation of philosophers: "If in the future I ever meet a philosopher I

will get out of his way as if he were a mad dog." And Lycinus' final advice in Lucian is also very much in line with the present ending: "You will do better in the future to make up your mind to join in the common life and share in the every-day life of the city."

These things were said by them. "How then, you men of Greece, can it be safe for those who desire to be saved to fancy that they can learn the true religion from these philosophers who are neither able so to convince themselves as to prevent sectarian wrangling with one another, and not to appear definitely opposed to one another's opinions?" Lucian is in a similar quandary in *Icar.*: "I put myself in the hands (of the philosophers) and then I expected to be taught how to hold forth on the the Heavens and to learn the system of the universe. But they plunged me forthwith into even greater perplexities by flooding me every day with first causes, final causes, atoms, voids, elements, concepts, and all that sort of thing. But, although no one of them agreed with anyone else in anything he said, but all their statements were contradictory and inconsistent, they nevertheless expected to persuade me and each tried to win me over to his doctrine." Di Pauli, *Die Irrisio*, pp. 2–4, gives a detailed account of the vacillations of earlier scholars concerning the date of the *Diasurmos*. His own view still sounds good (p. 53): "Wir glauben deshalb nicht irre zu gehen, wenn wie die Abfassung der *Irrisio* in den Zeitraum von 180–220 verlegen—als terminus a quo gilt Lucian, dessen Schriften ja Hermias wie wir nachgewiesen haben, sicher gekannt hat."

M. Martino, "Giustino martire di fronte ai probleme della metempsychosis" (*Dial.* 4, 4–7 e 5, 5). *Salesianum* 54 (1992) 231–81 finds the first patristic reference to metempsychosis in Justin, *Dialog.* chaps. 4 and 5, which thus may provide a *terminus a quo* for the date of the present work. Hanson's date is "environ a 200 ap. J. C." (p. 7). The question of date has also been raised by Kindstrand (1980) and Bauckham (1985). Bauckham thinks it is the work of a predecessor or contemporary of Clement of Alexandria.

In the opinion of the present writer, it is best located in the school of Origen. "This low jester, Celsus, omitting no species of mockery and ridicule which can be employed against us," (οὐδὲν δὲ εἶδος τοῦ περὶ ἡμῶν διασυρμοῦ καὶ καταγέλωτος καταλιπὼν ὁ βωμολόχος Κέλσος), *Contra Census*, 3, 22. And again: "Observe how this venerable philosopher like a low buffoon turns into ridicule and a subject of laughter and mockery," IV, 133–38 are particularly helpful. (εἰς χλεύην καὶ γέλωτα καὶ διασυρμόν).

One knows from the *Envoi* of Gregory Thaumatourgos, the wide curriculum Origen offered students in his school of philosophy. "He deemed those worthy to philosophize who with every energy had read all the writings of the ancient philosophers and singers, neither excluding nor disdaining any of them (since not yet able to discriminate) except those which belong to the atheists, who, since they have abandoned common human beliefs, say that there is no God or providence," tr. M. Slusser (*FOTC* 98, 1998) 116.

It should be urged in conclusion that a mere cataloging of Presocratic errors does not automatically disqualify Hermias from inclusion within the canon of early Christian apologists. Epiphanias much later still found it appropriate to do a very similar compilation of errors and contradictions in his *De fide* 9 (*PG* 42. 788–98; GCS 37 [Epiphanias 3] (Leipzig 1933) 505–9; Diels, *Dox*. 589–93). Theodoret, in the *Curatio*, and Augustine, *Civ. Dei* VIII.2 are in the same tradition.

We read in ps.-Justin, *Cohort. ad Graec.* 8: "It is logical, then, since you cannot learn any religious truths from your own teachers, whose ignorance is evident to you from their contradictions, to turn to our [Christian] forefathers." Judged by this two-tiered description of the early Christian apologetical enterprise, we can conclude that Hermias accomplishes something of a doxographical tour-de-force on the first part, but, as far as our surviving evidence goes, stops short of the second. To show disarray in the ranks of the philosophers, however, was the necessary clearing-ground in apologetic for the presentation of Christian revelation. It was also a useful school exercise for prospective philosophers and theologians. Once again one is reminded of Gregory

Thaumatourgos at the school of Origen.

BIBLIOGRAPHY

Alfonsi, L. "Aristotele in Ermia," Aevum 32 (1958) 380–85.

Bauckham, R. "The Fall of the Angels as the Source of Philosophy in Hermias and Clement of Alexandria," VigChr 39 (1985) 313–30.

Bonis, K. G. Theologia (Athenai) 60 (1989) 537–91.

Kindstrand, J. F. (1980) "The Date and Character of Hermias' 'Irrisio,'" VigChr 34, 1980, 341–57.

Paquet L., et al., Les Presocratiques Bibliographie Analytique, (1879–1980), 2 vols., (Paris 1988).

Thom, J. C. "The Journey Up and Down: Pythagoras in Two Greek Apologists," ChHist. 58 (1989) 299–308. [Ad Autol. 3,7, Irrisio, 16–17.]

Wyss, B. "Doxographie," RAC IV (1957–58) 197–210.

www.ingramcontent.com/pod-product-compliance
Lightning Source LLC
Chambersburg PA
CBHW061517040426
42450CB00008B/1661